Contents

Front cover illustration: View of the Monastery's south façade
Back cover illustration: Hall of Battles. The Monks' Garden from the Convalescents' Gallery.

PHILIP II, THE CATHOLIC MONARCHY AND EL ESCORIAL

The Monasterio de San Lorenzo de El Escorial is the monument which best sums up the ideological and cultural aspirations of the Spanish "Golden Age". It belongs to a period in which Spain became not only the champion of the Catholic Counter-Reformation against those countries which had embraced the cause of the Protestant Reformation but also, through the territorial possessions acquired by dint of its dynastic alliances in Europe and domination of virtually all of the known American continent, the greatest of all the world powers. The "Catholic King's" struggle for hegemony in Europe, his defence of the traditional religion and the cult of his dynasty and person as God's elect, were expressed in El Escorial through a highly original synthesis of Italian and Flemish artistic forms.

The founder of El Escorial was Philip II (1527-1598), King of Spain and the Indies, and of Naples, Sicily, Milan and the Netherlands, all ceded to him by his father, the Emperor Charles V, who abdicated in 1556 and withdrew to the Monastery of Yuste, where he was to die in 1558. Charles V was a key figure in the foundation of El Escorial for it was he who most influenced his son through the example of his last years among the Hieronymite monks of Yuste, impressing on Philip the need to provide him with a worthy tomb. The defeat of Henry II of France at the battle of St Quentin on 10th August 1557 – the first great military victory of Philip's reign – coincided with the feast of St Lawrence ("San Lorenzo")

– which explains, at least in part, the monastery's dedication.

Enriched with the contributions made to it by each successive monarch, the Monastery continued to function according to its founder's designs and wishes until 1835. Philip III ordered the construction of the Royal Pantheon, completed by Philip IV, who ordered the installation of a large number of paintings which, from 1656, were chosen and positioned by Velázquez himself. Charles II ordered the Monastery rebuilt after the fire of 1671 and added the sacristy *altarpiece*, which thereafter displayed Claudio Coello's masterpiece *The Adoration of the Holy Eucharist* and Luca Giordano's majestic series of *frescoes*. In 1767, Charles III ordered the construction of other buildings at the Royal Seat, including the new *Lonja*, the *Casita del Príncipe* and the *Casita del Infante*, and Charles IV ordered the alterations to the north façade, the decoration of the Bourbon Palace and the rich ornamentation of the *Casita del Príncipe*.

During the Napoleonic Wars the monastery's art collections suffered heavy losses (a situation in part redressed by the subsequent recovery of some works and the restoration of others by Ferdinand VII), while in the 19th century disentailment led to the dispersal of the Hieronymite community and the reversion of its assets to the crown. The monastery thereafter performed various religious functions until it was assigned to the Augustinians in 1885. The commemoration of the four hundredth anniversaries of the beginning and end of its construction in 1963 and 1986, and

(Opposite) Juan Pantoja de la Cruz, Philip II. *El Escorial Library*

of the death of Philip II in 1998 prompted works of restoration and new studies of El Escorial.

THE ARCHITECTURE

El Escorial cannot be considered the work of a single architect, but rather the result of a complex labour of collaboration whose most prominent figures were the architects Juan Bautista de Toledo and Juan de Herrera. A former assistant of Michelangelo's in the Vatican, Toledo was responsible for the general arrangement of the ground floor and most of its design, while Herrera took charge of most of the actual construction and with it of many other parts Toledo had not designed. However, taking into account the numerous consultations made with Italian and Spanish architects before a final synthesis was reached, El Escorial should rather be considered a very special manifestation of the character of Philip II.

Although various functions were performed under its roof, the Real Monasterio de San Lorenzo was essentially a monastery of monks of the order of St Jerome with the church a pantheon for the Emperor Charles V, his son Philip II, members of their families and successors and a place where the monks were charged to pray *ad perpetuum* for the souls of the royal personages interred there.

The palace provided accommodation for the King and his retinue, while the college and seminary fulfilled the religious functions, and the library served the three. All is laid out within a large rectangle with the sacred area containing the church and its atrium at the centre. Above the atrium vestibule is the library. To the right stands the monastery itself, arranged around one large court and four small ones, while to the left are the outbuildings of the king's palace and the college. Behind the church and projecting out of the rectangle is the *Casa del Rey*.

Juan Bautista de Toledo's "universal design" was influenced by the cruciform ground plans of the Italian and Spanish hospitals of the 15th century, but his main source of inspiration was the traditional layout of the mediaeval monasteries. The complex is orientated to the four cardinal points with the altar facing east. On that side and to the south, where the land drops, it is bordered by gardens supported by strong walls. On the north and west sides, where the terrain is higher, it is surrounded by the *Lonja*. As one reaches the end of the rise, the most picturesque side of the building – the *Casa del Rey* and the rear wall of the basilica with its dome – is revealed. It is necessary to walk the entire length of the *Lonja* and round the building to reach the *main façade*. Although the building's uniformity and severity are imposing, each façade has a character of its own.

Such uniformity was hardly in keeping with Toledo's original idea for the building, as he intended the west half to rise one floor less and towers to rise at the highest points of the north and south façades.

In 1564 Philip II decided to enlarge the building, making it four storeys high, and he increased the number of monks from fifty to one hundred.

Having resolved to found the monastery, in 1558 Philip began to

(Opposite) Copy by Johanes Blaeu of Juan de Herrera's design (1672).

consider where it should be sited, reaching a decision late in 1562. Following Juan Bautista de Toledo's project, the monastery was practically finished by 1571 and in 1572 the *Casa del Rey* was begun. Work on the basilica began in 1574 and ended in 1586. Although the last stone had been laid in 1584 and the decoration had taken several years more, the basilica was consecrated in 1595, which can be considered the year of its completion. The King supervised the work personally, holding the architect, the prior and two committees responsible for it. The architect answered directly to the King, who had appointed him personally, rather than to the prior, who in all other ways took all key decisions and headed the "congregation", an executive committee in charge of all legal and financial aspects, inspection and payments.

The *main façade* has three entrances, those at the sides – the left leading to the college and the right to the monks' area – being identical. At the centre, the *main portal* leads to the monastery and the basilica. It therefore has a religious character unrelated to the adjacent building, which is the *library*, but it is related to the church, whose true main façade rises at the end of the atrium. The royal coat of arms and statue of *St Lawrence* were carved by Juan Bautista Monegro.

THE CHURCH

At the end of the *vestibule*, the *Kings' Courtyard* is dominated by the great *dome* and the *basilica façade*. The *sculptures* of the six great kings of Judah in the first section were also carved by Monegro. The tower on the right is known as the "clock" or "bell" tower, while that on the left is the "small bell" tower, its name coming from the Flemish carillon (reinstalled in 1988) which it originally housed.

The great conventual church is El Escorial's true *raison d'être*. Although Juan Bautista de Toledo set its position and boundaries within his universal design, it was not actually his project that was implemented but rather a synthesis from which Juan de Herrera took advantage of a number of different ideas. Toledo's project consisted of a semi-circular apse flanked by towers but the architect and engineer Francesco Paciotto criticized its general proportions in 1562 and submitted another project with a square church the following year. Although Toledo drew new plans in 1567, Philip II ordered a collection of designs by the best Italian architects also to be assembled. In 1572 these were vetted together with the Spanish plans by the Academy of Fine Arts in Florence and Vignola in Rome. When Philip examined them in 1573, he declared them all of little use. He continued to hesitate but in 1574 finally decided on what apparently was Herrera's preference for Paciotto's plans.

The Basilica consists of two churches; an area before the choir for the congregation – called the *sotacoro* – and the Royal Chapel and conventual church. The ground plan of the former reproduces on a smaller scale that of the church, its central area standing beneath a very bold *flat vault*. Altars to either side of the central arch were used to celebrate mass

(Opposite) The Lonja *and the Monastery's main façade.*

for the common people. Between this area and the Royal Chapel is the *seminarists' choir*, which is separated from the chapel by large bronze gates made by Guillén de Tujarón in Saragossa.

Above the *sotacoro* and at the same level as the main floor runs the *monks' choir* (closed to the public). The stalls were made by the Genoese Giuseppe Flecha and the organ cases by Enrique Cotén. One of the 124 stalls, which is slightly wider than the rest, was reserved for Philip II to follow the services from the choir. The *Glory* fresco on the vault was painted by Luca Cambiasso. The murals, which Cambiasso had not been able to begin by the time of his death, were painted by Romulo Cincinato.

Even before passing through the bronze gates it is possible to see the *sanctuary*, with the huge *High Altarpiece* at the back and the *royal cenotaphs* at the sides, all designed by Juan de Herrera in the classicist style. The entire gilt bronze group of sculptures was cast by the Milanese craftsmen Leone and Pompeo Leoni.

The lower section contains the beautiful *Tabernacle* niche designed by Herrera and built with several types of Spanish marble by Jacome da Trezzo between 1579 and 1586. The two canvases in the first section and the middle canvas in the second section were painted by Pellegrino Tibaldi, while the remainder are the work of Federico Zuccari.

The cenotaphs – Charles V's on the left or Gospel side and Philip II's on the right or Epistle side – are surmounted by the Kings' respective coats of arms. Of the three doors below each, those nearest the pulpit lead to the sacristy and relics chapel and the others to the small *oratories* adjacent to the kings' bedrooms, in an arrangement emulating that in the Emperor's quarters at Yuste. It can be said that Philip II actually slept above his future tomb and prayed beneath the place intended for his own orant sepulchral statue. He is surrounded by the figures of his wives Elizabeth of France, Mary of Portugal (mother of Don Carlos, who is next to her) and Anna of Austria. Opposite, and next to a Charles V in armour and arrayed in the imperial mantle, are the Empress Isabella (Philip II's mother) with, behind them, their daughter Maria and the Emperor's sisters, Mary of Hungary and Eleonore of France.

Like the vault in the choir, the *presbytery vault*, which displays the *Coronation of the Virgin*, is painted with frescoes by Cambiasso. The remaining vaults were faced with stucco in the 16th century, but in 1693 Charles II commissioned Luca Giordano to adorn them with the magnificent series of Baroque frescoes. Giordano is known in Spanish as "Lucas Jordán", his name castilianized due to the many pictures he painted for Spanish clients when in Italy and during his long years in Spain. The ease and speed with which he worked earned him the very apt nickname "Fa Presto" – "Luca works quickly" – and he painted these vaults and that above the monastery staircase in the space of just 22 months.

The two great altar-reliquaries at the end of the side-aisles display paintings of the *Annunciation* and *St Jerome in the*

(Opposite) The cenotaph of Philip II in the Basilica sanctuary.
(Pages 10-11) View of the Monastery from Mount Abantos.

Wilderness by Federico Zuccari, while almost forty other altarpieces in the chapels and niches contain canvases painted by the Spaniards Juan Fernández de Navarrete, Diego de Urbina, Luis de Carvajal and Alonso Sánchez Coello, and the Italians Luca Cambiasso, Romulo Cincinato and Pellegrino Tibaldi, among others.

The adornment of the Basilica is completed by two large bronze candelabra wrought by J. Simon of Antwerp c. 1571 and two pulpits which Manuel de Urquiza was commissioned to make for Ferdinand VII.

In one of the chapels at the east end of the church hangs a major work of 16th century Italian sculpture: the superb *Escorial Crucifix* of Carrara marble which Benvenuto Cellini carved between 1559 and 1562 for his own tomb in the Church of La Santissima Annunziata in Florence. This sculpture never reached its intended destination, however, for the Grand Duke of Tuscany persuaded Cellini to allow him to purchase it so that he could present it to Philip II. It is signed and dated on the pedestal. The softness in the modelling of the semi-naked figure is admirable.

THE PANTHEONS

Philip II conceived of El Escorial as a burial place for the kings and queens of Spain but it was to perform such a function only after his death. However he is reported as having said that he had built it as "a mansion for God", declaring that his son – if he so desired – could subsequently make it a mansion for his own mortal remains and those of his parents. The two pantheons belong to different centuries and so reflect very different aesthetic styles: the *Royal Pantheon* is Baroque and dates from the 17th century, while the eclectic *Princes' Pantheon* dates from the 19th century.

The *Royal Pantheon* is an octagonal chamber surmounted with a semi-dome. Herrera originally intended it to be built of granite only, but when Philip III decided to convert it into a pantheon in 1617, he instructed his "superintendent of royal works", Giovanni Battista Crescenzi, to face it with marble and bronze according to a design by Juan Gómez de Mora. Work continued into the reign of Philip IV and the pantheon was completed in 1654.

Crescenzi commissioned the bronze decoration with Italian craftsmen, most of whom were Genoese, while the marble-work was executed by Pedro de Lizargárate and Bartolomé Zumbigo the Elder. During the reign of Philip IV certain technical difficulties were encountered, such as flooding caused by an underground spring when the floor level was being lowered, and various alterations were made, including the embellishment of the dome with grotesques, the installation of the new floor, the facing of the staircase and its doorways, the gilding of the bronze-work and the addition of further bronze pieces. The richness of the bronze and marble, the pomp of the Corinthian order and the exuberance of the grotesques make this chamber a noteworthy example of Italian early-Baroque art – a version more international than its Hispanic

(Opposite) Benvenuto Cellini, The Escorial Crucifix.

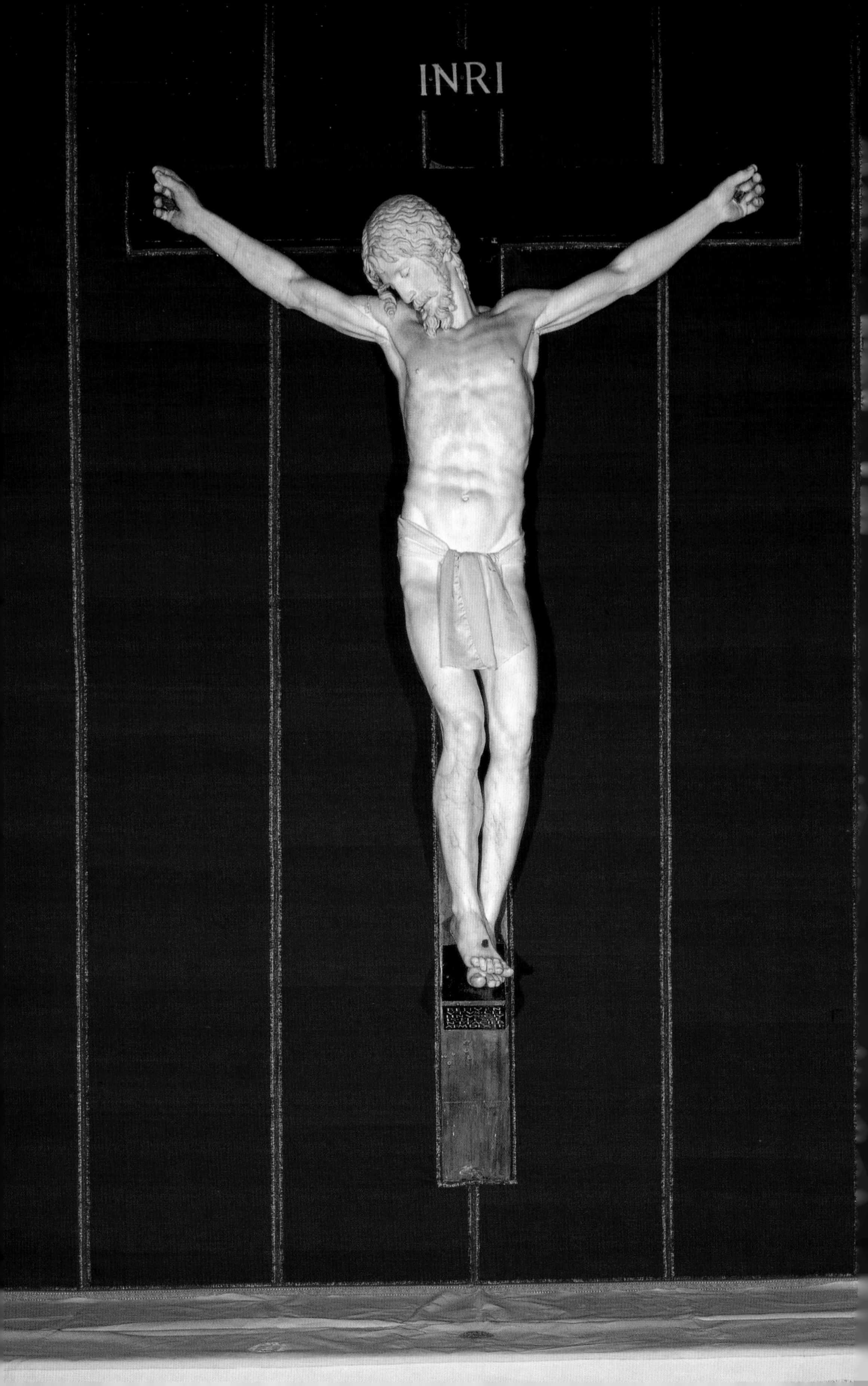
I·N·R·I

counterpart. The altar is dominated by a *Christ Crucified* carved by Domenico Guidi, a sculptor less well-known than Pietro Tacca and Gian Lorenzo Bernini, but more fortunate for Tacca's and Bernini's earlier crucifixes for the chamber are now situated in the sacristy and college chapel.

On a monarch's death (one prerequisite for the inclusion of queens was that of having given birth to a king) the body was placed in the *pudridero* – a kind of temporary vault adjacent to the tomb – where it was allowed to decompose, and after a number of years the remains were placed in urns. The kings' urns are on the right-hand side of the altar in chronological order, from Charles V to Alfonso XIII, and the queens' on the left. Only the remains of Philip V, his son Ferdinand VI and their wives are absent as they wished to be buried in their respective foundations at La Granja de San Ildefonso and the Monastery of Las Salesas Reales in Madrid.

Completed in 1888, the *Princes' Pantheon* was built in the reign of Isabella II according to plans by José Segundo de Lema. Each of the nine chambers beneath the sacristy and the Chapter Rooms is faced with marble and contains an altar. The sculptures and decorative motifs were carved in Carrara marble by Jacopo Baratta di Leopoldo after designs by the Aragonese Ponciano Ponzano. Inspired by historicist sources, the style of the pantheon gave rise to a number of new forms of truly sepulchral gravity. The cold richness of the marble, its colour, the pantheon's historical relevance, and the 19th century spirit permeating the site all make it well worth visiting.

Particularly important in the *first chamber* are a Neo-Classical altar with a *Descent from the Cross* by Carlo Veronese, and the tombs of the infantas Josefa Amalia of Saxony (designed by Isidro González Velázquez), the infanta Luisa of the Two Sicilies (with an orant of her daughter-in-law, Isabella II), and the Duke and Duchess of Montpensier and their daughters (designed by Aimé Millet). The *fifth chamber* contains the historicist tomb of *Don Juan de Austria*, built by Giuseppe Galeotti after plans by Ponzano. The *sixth chamber* is a mausoleum for infantes who died before reaching puberty. Here the altar displays *Our Lady of the Veil*, a fine painting by Lavinia Fontana (1589). The *ninth chamber* has the greatest historical significance as it contains sixteen tombs of Spanish Habsburgs.

THE MONASTERY

Linked with the Monks' Garden, the Monastery occupies the whole south side of the building. The entrance is reached via a vestibule on the ground floor of the Basilica bell-tower which leads to the *Sala de la Trinidad*, a room named after a painting of the *Holy Trinity* by José de Ribera which once hung there. The canvas now displayed is an old copy of Ribera's original (which is now in the Museo del Prado). This area leads to the main cloisters, whose walls were covered with an extensive series of scenes from the *Redemption* by Pellegrino Tibaldi (1527-1596). This theme – among the most commonly depicted at El Escorial – is continued on the Main Staircase, where

(Opposite) Luca Giordano, The Glory of the Spanish Monarchy.
(Pages 16-17) The Royal Pantheon.

some of the scenes were painted not by Tibaldi but by Luca Cambiasso (1527-1585). The triptychs of the "stations" or processional altars at the four corners of the cloisters were painted between 1587 and 1590 by Luis de Carvajal (1556-1607), Romulo Cincinato (1540-1597), Tibaldi and Miguel Barroso (c. 1538-1590).

As the principal means of access to the Monastery, the staircase is richly embellished with mural paintings which include *The Glory of the Spanish Monarchy* (on the vault) and three scenes from the *Battle of St Quentin* plus one of *The Construction of the Monastery of El Escorial* (on the four friezes). These were all painted by the Neapolitan Luca Giordano (1634-1705) for Charles II during the improvements made to the Monastery in the wake of the fire of 1671.

At the centre of the cloister garden, which is known as the Evangelists' Courtyard and was designed as a "mystical earthly paradise", stands Juan de Herrera's famous temple. The statues of the Evangelists were carved by Juan Bautista Monegro, the four fountains being an allusion to the four rivers of Eden and the life-giving quality of the four Gospels.

A number of the monastery's main rooms overlook the cloisters: the Church of Prestado, which served as a chapel and pantheon for royal personages until the consecration of the Basilica, whose altar displays Titian's magnificent *Martyrdom of St Lawrence*; the two Chapter Rooms, the common vestibule and the Prior's Cell (all of which were intended, from the time of the monastery's foundation to serve as galleries of religious paintings), whose walls are graced by major works of art

including *The Crowning with Thorns* by Hieronymus Bosch, *St Jerome Penitent* by Titian, *The Allegory of the Holy League* by El Greco, *The Ecstasy of St Francis* by Ribera and *Joseph's Bloody Coat brought to Jacob* by Velázquez; and the Ante-Sacristy and Sacristy, whose vaults are painted with grotesques in the manner of the typical Italian Renaissance palace.

THE LIBRARY

It was Philip II's wish to assemble a royal library both superior to that in the Vatican and representative of his cultural and scientific interests. Acting on the advice of his most scholarly counsellors he considered the creation of a library based on Classical tradition whose holdings should not only include books but also all kinds of scientific objects and devices, such as celestial and terrestrial globes, mathematical instruments and spheres, and medals and coins. Due to its ever increasing importance and also for architectural reasons, the Library was finally relocated at the Basilica entrance in the second most important area of the complex.

Pellegrino Tibaldi was commissioned to adorn the Library with frescoes and with his assistants he depicted *The Seven Liberal Arts*, the stories and personages associated with them, and also representations of *Philosophy* and *Theology*.

Placed between the bookcases of fine wood, which were installed between 1589 and 1592, are portraits of Charles V, Philip II and Philip III by Juan Pantoja de la Cruz, and of Charles II by Juan Carreño

(Opposite) The Evangelists' Courtyard.
(Pages 22-23) View of the Library.

de Miranda. The books were placed on the shelves in a highly original manner, with the gilded inner edges facing outwards so that the title (engraved on each one) was displayed in such a way as to "make the whole room beautiful, for from floor to ceiling all is either painted or covered with gold".

In the course of his reign Philip II acquired a huge collection of books and manuscripts for the Library, making it one of the most important in 16th century Europe. The books in Latin include St Augustine's *De Baptismo Parvulorum*, a Beatus of Liébana manuscript, a *Codex Aureus*, a collection of manuscripts by St Isidore of Seville, and an assortment of beautifully illuminated missals and books of hours. Those in Castilian include the works of Alfonso X the Wise (*Cantigas de Santa María, Libro de los Juegos*), two codices on *Hunting* by Alfonso XI, *The History of Troy*, a *Ceremonial for the Coronation of the Kings of Castile and Aragon*, a collection of mediaeval bibles and several papers with the signature of St Teresa of Ávila.

Among the jasper and porphyry tables at the centre of the room are various scientific instruments, including Antonio Santucci's armillary sphere (16th century) and Tycho Brahe's celestial and terrestrial globes (17th century).

THE *CASA DEL REY*

Philip II's private palace extends eastwards beyond the main rectangle and around the Mascaroon Courtyard in a series of galleries which lead to official rooms and the King and Queen's private chambers. The arrangement and decoration of these rooms was always simple, for Philip's wish, on founding the Monastery, was to use it – in the mediaeval tradition – not only as a residence but also as a place of withdrawal into religious devotion.

The "guard room" and audience chamber in the north section form the areas intended for official occasions. The former contains the litter used by Philip in his last years. The latter is now known as the "Portraits Room", as it contains a series of likenesses of the Spanish Habsburg kings from Charles V (Charles I of Spain) to Charles II which were painted by the most prominent court portraitists of the age, among these Sir Anthony More, Alonso Sánchez Coello, Pantoja de la Cruz and Carreño de Miranda. The adjacent area forms part of the King's private apartments. Situated at the east end of this part of the palace is a gallery adorned with paintings of battles where Philip could walk when he so desired. To the south, the ante-chamber or "Royal Dining Room" is adorned with a comprehensive series of paintings of Philip's palaces and royal houses in the area around Madrid.

In an arrangement emulating that designed by Charles V for his "apartments" at Yuste, the King's and Queen's private chambers are situated to either side of the high altar in the Basilica, being connected directly with it by the Oratory, while a view of the gardens is provided by the windows of the largest room. Both areas currently contain similar devotional adornment as well as a

(Opposite) Philip II's private apartments. A folding chair (top left), a clock (top right), and the King's Bedroom viewed from the Study (bottom).

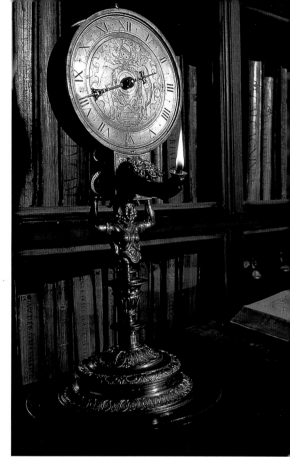

number of portraits of the family of
Philip II. The walls of the King's Study
continue to be graced by the plates with
drawings of animals and plants (some
attributed to Dürer) Philip was so fond of.

The Queen's Staircase leads not only to
the rooms in the Palace of Philip II but
also to the Hall of Battles on the same
level as the Monastery's main floor.
Judging by the mural paintings of Spanish
victories, such as the Battle of Higueruela
in the 15th century, various scenes of the
war between Spain and France, and the
Spanish naval campaign in the Azores
over the Portuguese succession during the
reign of Philip II, this area in the royal
chambers must have played a crucial part
in the projection of the King's image.

THE BOURBON PALACE

The Bourbon Palace occupies the north
and east sides of the first floor overlooking
the Palace Courtyard. In the reign of
Philip II it contained the chambers of the
infantes and other royal personages. In
the reign of Charles III work began to
convert the area into apartments for the
Prince and Princess of Asturias, the future
Charles IV and his wife Maria Luisa of
Parma. On ascending the throne, they
continued to reside there and ordered the
royal architect Juan de Villanueva to
make further changes, including a new
arrangement for the north façade and the
construction of a new staircase. It was in
the rooms intended for use in the autumn
where the practice in Spanish palaces
(initiated during the reign of Philip V) of
framing tapestries with wooden

mouldings to form fixed adornments
reached its height with Charles III and
Charles IV.

This palace is one of the best-preserved
examples of decorative art from the
Bourbon period. The items displayed in its
rooms are extremely interesting, as they
include important pieces produced
exclusively for the crown by the great
royal factories founded especially for this
purpose. Particularly outstanding is the
splendid collection of tapestries, most of
which were woven at the Santa Bárbara
Royal Factory. The cartoons for them were
painted by the most prominent court
artists of the 18th century, including
Andrés de la Calleja, Antonio González
Ruiz, Antonio González Velázquez and
Guillaume Anglois, all of whom worked at
the factory in the 1750s and '60s
producing scenes based on popular
themes. From the 1770s scenes of hunting
and of life in Madrid were also produced
and the artists who painted the cartoons
included Francisco de Goya, José del
Castillo and Ramón Bayeu.

As regards furniture, most of the
pieces were produced by the Spanish
royal workshops in the Neo-Classical
(late 18th century) and Empire (early
19th century) styles. The major porcelain
collection consists mainly of vases
produced in Paris in the 19th century,
although there are also a number of
noteworthy items made at the Royal
Factory in Naples in the late 18th century.
Another interesting collection consists of
timepieces, mostly of French manufacture
and generally in the Empire style,
although others date from the last third of
the 18th century and there are a few

clocks from the same period which are English. There are also a number of magnificent lamps from the Royal Glass Factory at La Granja.

THE MUSEUMS

The area containing the Museums is reached by crossing the "Halls of Honour", two rooms on the east side of the main courtyard which formerly led to the royal chambers. These contain the Monastery's extremely interesting collection of 16th century Flemish tapestries as well as El Greco's famous painting *The Martyrdom of St Maurice*.

The Architecture Museum is housed in one gallery and six large vaulted rooms. It contains models and drawings illustrating the history of the building and the various stages in its construction as well as copies (the originals being in the Palace Library) of Juan Bautista de Toledo's and Juan de Herrera's plans and Perret's engravings for the Monastery. Exhibited in the second room are sets of tools from various trades, most of which are engraved with St Lawrence's gridiron. Also displayed are machines and devices used in the Monastery's construction, including the great claw which lifted the stones by a system of wheels and pulleys.

In Philip II's old Summer Palace nine exhibition rooms contain most of El Escorial's collection of mainly 16th and 17th century paintings by the Spanish, Italian and Flemish schools. Particularly important from the Spanish school are a number of works by José de Ribera (*St Jerome Penitent*), Francisco Zurbarán (*The*

Presentation of the Virgin in the Temple) and one of Philip II's favourite artists, Juan Fernández de Navarrete (*The Beheading of St James*). From the Italian school are paintings by Titian (*St Margaret*), Tintoretto (*The Adoration of the Shepherds*), Veronese (*The Annunciation*), Palma the Younger (*The Baptism of Christ*), Il Guercino (*Lot and His Daughters*), Guido Reni (*St Monica and St Augustine*) and Luca Giordano (*The Martyrdom of St Justina*). Representing the Flemish school are Rogier van der Weyden's magnificent *Calvary*, a whole room dedicated to the work of Michel Coxcie, and two *flower vases* by Daniel Seghers.

THE AREA AROUND THE MONASTERY: THE GROUNDS. THE *CASITAS*

The buildings around the *Lonja*, which were erected to serve the Palace and Monastery in the 16th and 17th centuries, were not included in Juan Bautista de Toledo's original plans for the complex. Opposite the north façade, which was remodelled in the 18th century by Villanueva, stand two houses built by Herrera in the 16th century to accommodate the king's servants. At the southwest end of the *Lonja* is the *Compaña*, built for the monks in the late 16th century by Francisco de Mora and connected to the monastery by an arched gallery. Until the reign of Charles III no other buildings of any great importance existed around the Monastery: the main façade faced the mountains in a dialogue between art and nature and the Hieronymite monks lived like hermits

(Opposite) El Greco, The Martyrdom of St. Maurice.

devoting themselves to prayer in the wilderness.

The remaining buildings around the Lonja thus date from the 18th century and were raised by Juan de Villanueva on the orders of Charles III. While retaining the spirit of El Escorial, Villanueva fell back on his Italian classicist training, the result, in addition to the *Compaña*, being the long *Casa de Infantes* (begun in 1771), with, at right-angles to it, the *Casa del Ministro del Estado* (completed in 1785).

At the end of the main façade and at the foot of the *Lonja* steps a gallery links the Monastery with the *Compaña*. Below it a doorway opens onto the Pharmacy Courtyard, at the end of which stands the Convalescents' Gallery, built by Juan Bautista de Toledo. In addition to being a form of architectural ornamentation for the retaining wall between the different levels of the *Lonja* and the garden, the gallery's "sunlit corridors" served, as the name suggests, as rest areas for ailing monks.

The Monks' Garden lies within an esplanade that is supported by strong walls and serves as a platform for the Monastery; pairs of steps lead down to the *garden*, which is dominated by a beautiful pond designed by Francisco de Mora.

The path below the gallery running to the *Compaña* leads to the *Casa de Arriba* or *Casita del Infante*, built between 1771 and 1773 by Juan de Villanueva for Charles III's son, the infante Don Gabriel. This noble Ionic building is surrounded by a garden terraced in the Italian style which affords one of the best views of the Monastery. It is open to the public every

day during Holy Week and the summer months except Mondays.

Based on Palladian models, the building is designed around a central two-storey hall which served as an auditorium for concerts of chamber music. Typical of Villanueva's style is the large entrance space with columns framed by stone masses.

Finally, a pathway leads down from the Monastery's north façade through a fenced park to the *Casita de Abajo* or *Casita del Príncipe*, built by Villanueva at the same time as the *Casita de Arriba* for Don Gabriel's elder brother, the future Charles IV. It is not only larger than the *Casita de Arriba* but the decoration inside is also in a better state of conservation. The "Pompeian" ceilings were painted by Vicente Gómez, Manuel Pérez, Juan de Mata Duque and Luigi Japelli, and those of stucco, in the Neo-Classical style, were designed by Giambattista Ferroni. Of religious, allegorical and mythological themes, the pictures were painted mainly by the Neapolitans Luca Giordano and Corrado Giaquinto.

Like the *Casita del Infante*, the problem posed by the difference in level between the main and ancillary buildings is admirably solved (in this case in a more complicated manner), as is that of the relationship between the building and the area around it. Villanueva enlarged the building on the orders of the Prince between 1781 and 1784, adding the large hall and the oval room (which forms the current "T" shape), the pond and the upper terrace of the garden, which is dominated by the Basilica's dome as it rises up among the treetops in the park.